# Radio In the Night

*poems by*

# Judith Chibante

*Finishing Line Press*
Georgetown, Kentucky

# Radio In the Night

Copyright © 2017 by Judith Chibante
ISBN 978-1-63534-099-0 First Edition
All rights reserved under International and Pan-American Copyright Conventions.
No part of this book may be reproduced in any manner whatsoever without written permission from the publisher, except in the case of brief quotations embodied in critical articles and reviews.

## ACKNOWLEDGMENTS

"Thank you" to the editors of the following publications in which some of these poems first appeared, some in slightly different form:

*Tule Review*: Tomato Summers, Morning Devotions, These Redwoods Growing So Magnificently Here
*Song of the San Joaquin*: Turkey Dust Mornings, The Quonset Hut, 1952, Radio In the Night, Always Dinner
*Survivor's Review*: December
Ina Coolbrith Circle anthology, *The Gathering 11*: Sunday Afternoon Visits to Elderly Relatives

With deep gratitude to, and unabashed admiration for, my teacher, Ellen Bass.

Publisher: Leah Maines

Editor: Christen Kincaid

Cover Art: Phyllis Scott Johnson

Author Photo: Berta Gonzalez

Cover Design: Elizabeth Maines

Printed in the USA on acid-free paper.
Order online: www.finishinglinepress.com
also available on amazon.com

Author inquiries and mail orders:
Finishing Line Press
P. O. Box 1626
Georgetown, Kentucky 40324
U. S. A.

# Table of Contents

## I

Tomato Summers ................................................................... 1
Turkey Dust Mornings .......................................................... 2
Morning Devotions ................................................................ 3
The Quonset Hut, 1952 ......................................................... 4
Sunday Afternoon Visits To Elderly Relatives ..................... 5
Swans In a Mahogany Frame ............................................... 6
My Father's Hands ................................................................. 7
Always Dinner ........................................................................ 9
Finished Business ................................................................. 10
Cutting Peaches .................................................................... 11
Letter To Mary ...................................................................... 12
To an Unknown Grandfather .............................................. 14

## II

Phone Call During Dinner .................................................. 17
December .............................................................................. 18
Walking Back Alleys ............................................................ 19
Letter After Cancer .............................................................. 20
These Redwoods Growing So Magnificently Here ........... 21
Radio In the Night ............................................................... 22

*To CR*

I

**Tomato Summers**

Summers hung thick and low
over our mother's vegetable garden.
Sun-burnished gems sagged on green-spun
vines, huge dollops of crimson
that we'd gather up in over-sized tin pails.
We slept the short, sweat-filled nights
under the ruby dusk of their fragrance, dreamt
dark dreams about mushroom clouds
and ashes of death, as night
stretched above the sleeping porch
where we lay open to the sky.

It's the sixties, and it's all of us—the kids
of long summers, earth-dipped heat,
afternoons in the irrigation ditch.
Lunchtime meant tomato sandwiches:
we slathered the mayo on home-made bread,
cut fat slices of purple onion,
turned on *Rock 'n Roll KYNO Radio*,
its news-on-the-hour full of nuclear tests, ICBMs,
reviews of the Emergency Broadcast System.

We gave away tomatoes by double-
bagged sacks—to friends in the church,
the Mendoza family across the road,
the Souzas building a bomb shelter
under their dairy barn. Still we unloaded
the earth of its scarlet weight, as we ate
the red flesh of summer
and looked for the world to end.

## Turkey Dust Mornings

We'd wake up to bleary sunlight,
stand by the side of the crooked farm road—
country kids waiting for the school bus. Past
the swells of pasture a broad trailing cloud
hung low over the ground, a thickening
brown broth with a thousand restless turkeys
at its heart, astir in early day to feed
in the open spaces of
their pens.

*It's a turkey dust morning*
Dad would say.

We smelled it, a musky scent of manure,
hay and feed, could see in the air bits
of feather, fine particles of mash, crazed
gnats and flies glancing off each other. We blinked
through the grit, worked to breathe
in the muffled silence, gagged on the gritty
feral air. Then sound first

of a toiling diesel engine, a shape
through the haze became the sleek
yellow hulk of bus come to take us
to another world where we knew no one
would believe us:

that out here in the country
fog could come from something other
than the earth as it cools, or the ocean
giving itself up to air.

## Morning Devotions

Every morning after breakfast
my sisters and I read aloud from the family Bible,
then bowed our heads over empty dishes
as Dad lead us in prayer. His elbows were fixed on the table,
huge, burled hands over his eyes, his voice low and full
as he prayed, always, for the lost souls in foreign lands,
that they would learn of their sins. And he prayed
for Chelo in Uruguay, the Jantzens in Appalachia, for all
the martyrdom-willing missionaries
working to save a wicked world.

To go to the mission fields was Dad's highest hope for us.
But with eyes closed, listening to his fervor,
I'd see the book on our living room shelf,
*Judith, Martyred Missionary of Russia*—
her body a blackened stump in burnt ruins.
I had reread the final scene countless times—
this book with my own name on every page, fixed
to a lurid mutilation. As the smells of bacon and toast
faded in the closed air, Dad prayed last for us.
*In Jesus' name, Amen.* Then we'd check the clock,
push back from the checkered oilcloth, rush
for the school bus. And not the press of my classmates
all those slow morning rides, nor the passing countryside
of cows and pastures, the unhurried canals curving
across open fields, could save me from the vision
of a long, scorching death, carried out by a heathen people
deaf to my cries.

## The Quonset Hut, 1952

We came across it one day while exploring
the old naval airport. Heaped to its water-stained,
tin ceiling was a mountain of comic books:
hundreds? thousands? They smelled
delicious: damp and mold, stale smoke.

Lying among them with my sisters,
I first met Archie and big-breasted, darkly beautiful
Veronica, felt the hidden manliness
of Clark Kent, the straight-edge honor
of Sergeant Preston and his loyal Mounties.
Whole afternoons stretched into evening,
chores and dinner forgotten.

Then one day we opened the slow, rusty door
and they were gone: dirt floor swept clear,
ragged sunlight giving back empty, dust-filled air.
All those bright champions, the wildly improbable,
happy endings: how would we go on without them
through a long, desolate summer?

## Sunday Afternoon Visits To Elderly Relatives

Their parlors always smelled of old age—
fusty air, a dull scent of lavender hanging heavily
over dark furniture. Worn, tatted doilies pinned
to chair arms and the backs of brocade settees.

I'd work to sit still, a loose sandal
keeping one foot busy, while the adults droned on.
The inquiries about who was ailing, who had died
floated over the yellowed keys of a faded
upright piano and a gnarled philodendron
sprawled in the corner.

When talk ran out, we'd leave by the front path,
past withered hydrangeas and tea-garden rose bushes.
We turned and waved good-bye to shadow persons
standing at the window. Then we'd drive back home.
And in my world of dolls, cats, and spreading
gum trees to climb,  I worked every day to forget
the dreary visited, vowing never to grow old.

## Swans In a Mahogany Frame

They drifted—a pair—on a shadowed stream,
oak and elm glinting gold
on the altar of an autumn afternoon.
White dollops, one with neck bowed, her mate
hovering, they swam the living room wall
above the sofa in my childhood home.
When I was sick, I lay below them,
slept in and out of their gaze.
Evenings, coming in from the fields,
Dad would stamp his dirt-filled boots
under their calm and silence.
And when I pounded out 'Fur Elise' at the piano,
stretched for 'Moonlight Sonata,'
I felt their patience, their faith.
All through the dark of grandparents' deaths,
the failed years of sweet potatoes,
they preened before us, their constant audience.
Who were they among us, strange
as visiting angels—two dabs
of paint on canvas behind hazy glass?

## My Father's Hands

Early so rough
these huge hands of strength,
farming, milking hands,
and me in his lap
taking first one
then the other,
cleaning his nails
while he read the newspaper,
grooming my love
into their flat broad beds.

These hands
that took me into the air
caressing the rudder
of the Piper cub
(we would float out
over the Gabilan hills), hands
knowing how to steer
and later moor the plane—
after the tie-down
they reached out to lead me
safe across the tarmac.

These hands measured
and sawed and pounded nails
in a single stroke,
built houses strong and sure
(all still standing)—
then gathered me up
at the end of long
carpenter days
for the ride back home.

Finally at rest,
having just flailed the air
and picked at worn bedsheets—
these
my father's hands.

**Always Dinner**

Mom would come home
after work, drop her purse,
and fall wearily onto the bed,
her back curved to the open doorway.
This was quiet time:
piano practice done, we'd start
the potatoes on a slow boil.

She showed us how to plant
tomato starts, can apricots, peaches
in steamy kitchens. And she told us
the stories of nine children
in a house without food, a father
who preached on street corners
while pots and stomachs
went empty.

But we never went without.
She would rise from too-brief rest,
like Venus low in the evening sky,
and lean from the kitchen stool
to lace together salad, lay out
her homemade bread—
another meal for us, days fading
into months and years,
as we unrelentingly grew up,
then moved away.

**Finished Business**

The night my mother died, her sewing machine held
the just-finished pajamas for my birthday,
stacks of fabric for next projects nearby.  On her desk,
books and papers were in order, accounting ledgers open, ready
for her careful, accurate figures, the cautious weighing
of profit and loss.

The night my mother died, pots of sweetheart ivy on the back porch
nodded to the cat's grin moon, waited
for their morning watering by her hand.
Basement shelves bowed under their weight of canned bounty:
quarts of apricots, cucumber stuffed with dill weed,
dozens of pints of peach and plum jam.  Her garden lay
in the black stillness: well-tilled rows of pendulous
tomato vines, tied-up bean plants, wild spills
of squash and watermelon.

The night my mother died, her last casserole waited in the freezer,
to be served up on a July evening the night before her service.
Her closet was a muted rustle of simple, handmade clothes,
the dusky scent of Youth Dew alive in its close air.

The night my mother died, we held vigil and fed her
the merciful morphine, one slow dropper-full at a time.
We slept holding her hands, listening for her breath.  Then
we closed her eyes against the pink-pearl light of new day
cresting through her window.

**Cutting Peaches**

See the open shed, ragged in the melting mid-August sun.
Pickers in long sleeves, their faces swaddled in cloth masks,
dump boxes of golden-fuzzed, freestone peaches
onto the cutting tables. A thick fragrance fills the morning air,
an acrid smell of sulfur from the drying houses
not yet drifting in waves, burning eyes and throats.
It's a first job: slicing open peach, peach, peach—
one hand laying down halves on a slatted tray,
the other reaching, positioning the next peach for the full-circle
spin of blade. The sharper the knife, quicker your hands,
the faster trays fill with orbs of yellow flesh.
You're a country kid—lucky to get summer work on Mr. Miyaki's farm.
You ride an ancient bicycle for the 7 a.m. start time,
claiming a spot on the work line out of the drift of smoke,
away from the itchy drafts from row on row of trees.
At season's end, the raw, cut fingers, the slow hours of standing
convert to riches—a first paycheck, your breath gone
at money that is yours alone. And through the dust
of childhood, do you *feel* it?—how you've become
a gear in the huge engine of this life—the picking, cutting,
the laying out of the harvest?

## Letter To Mary

> *The ruins of the Great Depression included more than a million families abandoned to survive without husbands and fathers, men so devastated they could no longer lead normal lives.*

When your husband—
the grandfather I never knew—
left that late afternoon for a meeting in town,
I can't help but wonder: when did you know?
As you looked out on the gathering darkness,
strained to see through dust-weary blinds,
when did you move past
a prickle of worry—*Is he injured?*
*lying by the road?*—to a spreading apprehension:
that not this night, nor
in the next days or nights, would you hear
his footfall across the porch,
see in his eyes a stern devotion,
have him at your side to raise
four children?

I learned of your pain on summer visits,
along with how to grow kale, peanuts,
artichokes, how to wring tomato worms
in half (delicacies we lobbed
to the chickens). After collecting
the morning eggs, we'd go in to rest,
you on the big chair in the living room,
telling the story again, holding
your aging breasts, undressing them
for me (they looked just like
the butternut squash growing under
your kitchen window), while
you spoke of suckling babies
and the sins of mankind.

Years later when you moved into town,
you came to be known
in your long skirts and home-spun sweaters
as the wandering old woman of Merced,
sometimes seen as far downtown
as JCPenney. And when swollen,
ache-ridden knees, eyes shadowed white
by age, just barely slowed
your long days of plying the streets,
I came to believe you were looking—
searching—for him still.

## To an Unknown Grandfather

> *"I know this... a man got to do what he got to do."*
> John Steinbeck, *The Grapes of Wrath*

When the stranger strode across the greasy shop floor,
ignoring the blow torch in your hand, and spit out,
*Do you know who I am?*—did you fall back at darkened eyes
in a face so like your own? Maybe you thought
he wouldn't look for you—your grown child—when you fled
only as far as Berkeley, its iron shops near the water.
That night did you tell your wife
about the curious encounter with your past?
Did you tell her (anyone?) about Mary, speak
of the family you left behind?

I reread the few letters you sent my father
after he found you. Their postmarks say Faial,
the island of your birth in the Azores—and where you lived
in your last years. A final letter is here in this stash
of fragile paper shells, this one from your (second) wife.
She writes that your body was found half-way down
a sea cliff, the constable unsure of murder or suicide.
And though there's no remorse in your letters,
I imagine how you got on the bus one shattered winter's day.
You rode to the end of the line, hat pulled low,
coat closed against monstrous fingers of damp cold.
You picked your way past a wood railing and tugged
through the wind-bent underbrush. Then
a long step to the edge as the pulse of the ocean
grew alive in your veins. At last the black haunting
broke apart, as you pitched down
toward the sea's enfolding waves—its incessant tides.

II

**Phone Call During Dinner**

The truth is, I never saw
the fine mesh of porcelain,
the delicate pores
of the plates I held for years, extravagant
set from Rhodes Department Store,
a wedding gift two marriages ago.
But with the doctor's voice
in my ear, low, resonant, each word
exactly spoken, I see now
the pale scorch of kiln, scallops
of knife and time—and how
the single trail of cobalt along the rim
is perilously close
to careening into space.

## December

Every day I wore
a new pair of Christmas socks:
red and black with green puff-balls
around the cuffs, magenta
with holiday geese embroidered
in bright gold.
True, the crazy socks
were mostly hidden
under my jeans, but once
I lay down on the sterile table
for the next radiation, they were visible
to the efficient measurers
of exact photon dosage, to
the able technicians of check sheets
and reports. They could all see
the splashes of mad color
as they set about their grim task.
But not once did they mention them—
not when I wore the
navy-with-red-holly-berries, not
for the cherry-pink-and-gold-stars
with metallic threads that glistened
in the dim light.

**Walking Back Alleys**


Each day the arms move,
the legs reach out, a prescribed ritual to stay
the fatigue plundering my body
as I wrestle with the poison of radiation.
Here's a ragged garden with dirt-angled stakes
amid disheveled pots. Next a half-built playhouse,
weeds sprouting through a gaping low window.
And I wonder at the strange comfort
of witnessing grapevines tangled
around rose bushes, weeping arbors of wisteria
begging for light and air,
here in week six
of hiding from the world.

## Letter After Cancer

Emily, you were right.
Not that I doubted
as I learned your poem by heart.
But when it came down
to the diagnosis, the daily schedule
of radiation, it was hard to trust
that hope would stick around.
And when they spread cold plaster
on my face, fitted me
for the mask I'd wear each day,
I felt it might fly right out
of that sterile, windowless room.
So I'd like you to know: even
when my skin was charred black
and I left streams of hair
on the pillow each morning,
it was still here, Emily—
that great stab of a black bird,
ablaze.

## These Redwoods Growing So Magnificently Here

I was crazy, perhaps,
to go out and lay my hands
on the trees, to stroke their red shaggy trunks, ask
for their blessing, here in my new home,
freshly alone.

                    And I may have been a bit mad
to dig through a maze of roots, plant
begonias at their feet, to sleep naked
under their open branches, praying the beating air
hold, calm me.

                    But what I did wasn't half
as mad, half as crazy as the way
you left: a cocktail of pills, the long gash
of a Sunday morning siren.

                            So
I took the trees: their murmurs alive
through empty nights, the sighs of their spreading
limbs, the steamy musk of their rainfall scent—
these guardians who stood watch with me
at the reluctant start of a bare new life.

**Radio In the Night**

Dad brought it from his shop,
placed that small, brown square
with two button knobs, fabric
stretched over the round papery
speaker, on a low table
by my bed. He squatted down,
his six-foot-two frame rolled
into a plaid flannel ball, to show
how to find a clear station, keep
the volume low. It was a sweet box
of hushed company for me,
a terrified-of-the-dark child.

Through long nights as I lay
curled into cold sheets, blackness
pressing against the windows,
that radio reached out to me:
announcers with velvet tones,
singers tossing around jagged melodies
(my first hearing Ella), actors bringing
the Green Hornet, Superman,
The Shadow to life.

An equal darkness seeps now
into my father's brain, a black tide
filling up the interstices of memory,
the corn-ball humor. Outside his window,
yellow-stained maples grapple
with an early rain. The struggling light
of late afternoon brushes gray,
slow shapes across the wall.
I hold his hand as I read to him—
tonight, his favorite Psalms—a voice
in the gathering dark
as the last remnants of light
shut down around us.

**J**udith Chibante, cancer survivor, left a four-decade career in education to return to her creative writing roots. She was born and raised in rural California, and came of age in the sixties doing farmwork, strict religious practices, and sports in school. She left home at age 18 to go to college in southern California (an unforeseen, epic experience), and became just the second in her family to earn a degree.

From college, Judith went into teaching. Most of her experience was in a small high school as an English and remedial reading teacher. Later, she migrated to academia at a major university to work in teacher education; her specialty area was training teachers how to work with children having difficulty learning to read. In that role, Judith taught a daily case-load of hard-to-teach children in local schools. During this time, she edited a book of poems for teachers, and it was this project that helped take her back to poetry. To nurture a dormant aptitude, she sought special opportunities to work with established poets; for the past several years, she has studied with Ellen Bass in Santa Cruz.

Judith recently chaired the Berkeley Poetry Contest; several of her award-winning poems appear in this chapbook. Currently, she lives in Fresno, California, with her Tonkinese cat, Meisha, a rambling garden, and a small 'forest' of 9 redwoods (each named for a famous poet).

www.ingramcontent.com/pod-product-compliance
Lightning Source LLC
LaVergne TN
LVHW041516070426
835507LV00012B/1624